Keystrokes to Cash

Unlocking Six Figures from Home with Bookkeeping Brilliance

By
Robert J. White

Copyright Page:

Copyright © 2024 by Robert J. White

All rights reserved. No part of this book can be reproduced, distributed, or transmitted in any shape or with the aid of using any means, which includes photocopying, recording, or different digital or mechanical methods, without the prior written permission of the publisher, except in the case of brief quotations embodied in critical reviews and certain other noncommercial uses permitted by copyright law.

Disclaimer:

The facts supplied in this book are for instructional and informational functions only. While every effort has been made to ensure the accuracy and completeness of the information presented, the author and publisher make no representations or warranties of any kind, express or implied, about the completeness, accuracy, reliability, suitability, or availability concerning the contents of this book for any purpose. The information provided in this book is not intended to replace professional advice or guidance, and readers are encouraged to consult with qualified professionals before making any financial or business decisions.

Dedication:

This book is dedicated to all aspiring entrepreneurs and bookkeepers who dare to dream big and pursue their passions with courage and determination. May this book inspire and empower you to unlock your full potential and achieve your goals in the world of bookkeeping.

Table of content:

Copyright Page:
Disclaimer:
Dedication:
Table of content:
Introduction:
Chapter 1: The Foundation of Financial Fluency
section 1: Understanding the Basics of Bookkeeping
Section 2: Essential Accounting Principles Made Simple
Section 3: Setting Up Your Home Office for Success
Chapter 2: Mastering Money Management
Section 1: Tracking Income and Expenses Effectively
Section 2: Budgeting Techniques for Your Business and Clients
Section 3: Implementing Profitable Pricing Strategies
Chapter 3: Digital Dynamo: Leveraging Technology for Efficiency
Section 1: Exploring the Best Bookkeeping Software Solutions
Section 2: Automating Repetitive Tasks to Maximize Productivity
Section 3: Securing Data and Protecting Client Confidentiality
Chapter 4: Building Your Brand and Client Base
Section 1: Crafting a Compelling Brand Identity
Section 2: Marketing Strategies to Attract Ideal Clients

Section 3: Nurturing Long-Term Relationships for Referrals and Repeat Business
Chapter 5: From Keyboard to Cash: Managing Cash Flow Like a Pro
Section 1: Optimizing Cash Flow for Your Business and Clients
Section 2: Overcoming Common Cash Flow Challenges
Section 3: Strategies for Growth and Expansion
Chapter 6: Scaling Your Success: Going from Solo to Small Team
Section 1: Hiring and Training Assistants or Employees
Section 2: Delegating Tasks to Maintain Efficiency
Section 3: Managing Growth and Ensuring Quality Service
Chapter 7: Navigating Legal and Compliance Waters
Section 1: Understanding Tax Obligations for Your Business and Clients
Section 2: Compliance with Regulations and Standards
Section 3: Building a Strong Legal Foundation for Your Bookkeeping Business
Chapter 8: Beyond Bookkeeping: Diversifying Your Revenue Streams
Section 1: Exploring Additional Services to Offer Clients
Section 2: Creating Passive Income Opportunities
Section 3: Expanding Your Business Horizons
Chapter 9: Thriving in Turbulent Times: Adapting to Economic Shifts

Section 1: Strategies for Resilience During Economic Downturns
Section 2: Pivoting Your Business Model for Changing Needs
Section 3: Thriving in an Ever-Evolving Financial Landscape
Chapter 10: The Future of Bookkeeping: Trends and Innovations
Section 1: Embracing Technological Advancements in Bookkeeping
Section 2: Predicting Future Trends and Staying Ahead of the Curve
Section 3: Positioning Yourself as a Leader in the Industry
Conclusion:
Acknowledgments
About the Author

Introduction:

Welcome to the World of Bookkeeping Brilliance.

In the quaint town of Maplewood, nestled amidst rolling hills and whispering woods, there stood a modest cottage, its windows glowing warmly against the cool evening air. Inside, a figure hunched over a desk cluttered with papers and pens, their fingers dancing across the keyboard of a sleek laptop. This figure was none other than Emily Harris, a young woman with dreams as vast as the star-studded sky above her.

Emily wasn't just any ordinary dreamer; she was a visionary, with a burning desire to carve her path in the world of finance. From an early age, she possessed an uncanny knack for numbers, a gift passed down from her father, a seasoned accountant who regaled her with tales of balance sheets and ledgers.

Despite her passion, Emily found herself trapped in the monotony of a nine-to-five job, shackled to a desk in a dimly lit cubicle. But deep within her heart, she knew she was destined for something greater, something that would set her soul ablaze with purpose.

One crisp autumn morning, as the leaves painted the town in hues of gold and crimson, Emily made a decision that would change the course of her life forever.

With a determined gleam in her eye, she bid farewell to the confines of corporate life and embarked on a journey of entrepreneurship.

Armed with nothing but her wits and a thirst for knowledge, Emily dove headfirst into the world of bookkeeping. She devoured books and articles, and attended workshops and seminars, soaking up every ounce of wisdom like a sponge thirsty for water. And with each passing day, her confidence grew, her skills sharpened, and her vision crystallized into a clear and radiant beacon of hope.

But Emily's journey was not without its challenges. There were moments of doubt and uncertainty, where she questioned her decision to stray from the beaten path. There were sleepless nights spent poring over spreadsheets and reconciling accounts, her fingers numb from endless keystrokes. And there were setbacks and failures, the bitter taste of defeat lingering on her tongue like ashes.

Yet, through it all, Emily persevered. She refused to let fear or failure dictate her destiny, instead choosing to forge ahead with unwavering determination. And slowly however surely, her efforts commenced to bear fruit.

One client became two, two became four, and before she knew it, Emily found herself at the helm of a thriving bookkeeping business, her name whispered in hushed tones amongst the townsfolk. With each new success, she dared to dream bigger, to reach higher, and to unlock the secrets of financial freedom for herself and others.

And so, dear reader, it is with great pleasure and pride that I invite you to join Emily on her extraordinary journey—a journey filled with triumphs and tribulations, with laughter and tears, with moments of sheer brilliance and flashes of divine inspiration.

Within the pages of this book, you will discover the keys to unlocking six figures from the comfort of your own home, just as Emily did. You will learn the art of bookkeeping brilliance, honing your skills, and harnessing the power of technology to propel your business to new heights. You will uncover the secrets of financial fluency, mastering the language of money and wielding it like a seasoned maestro.

Above all, you will embark on a journey of self-discovery—a journey that will challenge you, inspire you, and empower you to embrace your inner brilliance and unleash your full potential upon the world.
So come, dear reader, and let us embark on this adventure together. The road ahead may be long and

winding, but with courage in our hearts and determination in our souls, there is no limit to what we can achieve.

Chapter 1: The Foundation of Financial Fluency

Welcome to Chapter 1 of your journey towards financial fluency, where we lay the groundwork for your success in the world of bookkeeping. In this chapter, we'll delve into the essentials of bookkeeping, demystify fundamental accounting principles, and guide you in setting up your home office for maximum productivity and success. So let's embark on this foundational journey together and equip you with the knowledge and tools you need to excel in the field of bookkeeping.

section 1: Understanding the Basics of Bookkeeping

Bookkeeping forms the cornerstone of financial management for businesses of all sizes, providing a systematic way to record, organize, and track financial transactions. In this section, we'll explore the fundamentals of bookkeeping and the key principles that underpin this essential discipline.

1.1 What is Bookkeeping?

At its core, bookkeeping is the process of recording, categorizing, and summarizing financial transactions of a business or organization. These transactions typically include sales, purchases, expenses, and other financial activities that occur in the course of business operations. The primary objective of bookkeeping is to maintain accurate and up-to-date records of these transactions, which serve as the foundation for financial reporting, analysis, and decision-making.

1.2 The Importance of Bookkeeping

Bookkeeping plays a vital role in the financial management of a business, providing the data and insights needed to make informed decisions, track performance, and ensure compliance with legal and regulatory requirements. By maintaining accurate and organized records of financial transactions, bookkeepers enable businesses to:

1. Track income and expenses: Bookkeeping allows businesses to monitor their cash flow, track revenue and expenses, and identify trends and patterns in financial performance.

2. Prepare financial statements: Bookkeepers prepare financial statements such as the balance sheet, income statement, and cash flow statement, which provide a snapshot of the business's financial position and performance.

3. Support tax compliance: Bookkeeping records serve as the basis for preparing tax returns and meeting tax obligations, ensuring compliance with tax laws and regulations.

4. Facilitate decision-making: Bookkeeping provides valuable insights into the financial health and performance of the business, enabling stakeholders to make informed decisions and strategic choices.

5. Enhance transparency and accountability: Accurate and transparent bookkeeping fosters trust and confidence among stakeholders, including investors, creditors, and regulatory authorities, by providing a clear and accurate picture of the business's financial affairs.

1.3 The Double-Entry Bookkeeping System

One of the foundational principles of bookkeeping is the double-entry bookkeeping system, which forms the basis for recording and balancing financial transactions. According to this system, every transaction affects at least two accounts, with one account debited and another account credited. The total debits must equal the total credits for each transaction, ensuring that the accounting equation (Assets = Liabilities + Equity) remains in balance.

1.4 Basic Bookkeeping Terms and Concepts

To navigate the world of bookkeeping effectively, it's essential to familiarize yourself with some basic terms and concepts:

1. Assets: Economic resources owned by the business, such as cash, inventory, equipment, and accounts receivable.
2. Liabilities: Obligations owed by the business to external parties, such as loans, accounts payable, and accrued expenses.
3. Equity: The residual interest in the assets of the business after deducting liabilities, representing the owner's or shareholders' stake in the business.
4. Revenue: Income earned from the sale of goods or services, representing the inflow of economic benefits to the business.
5. Expenses: Costs incurred in the course of business operations to generate revenue, such as rent, salaries, utilities, and supplies.
6. Accounts Receivable: Amounts owed to the business by customers or clients for goods or services provided on credit.
7. Accounts Payable: Amounts owed by the business to suppliers or vendors for goods or services received on credit.
8. General Ledger: A master record that contains all the accounts used by the business to record financial transactions, organized by account type and category.
9. Trial Balance: A summary of the balances of all accounts in the general ledger, used to verify that debits equal credits and that the accounting equation is in balance.

Section 2: Essential Accounting Principles Made Simple

Accounting principles provide the framework and guidelines for recording and reporting financial transactions accurately and consistently. In this section, we'll simplify some of the essential accounting principles that every bookkeeper should understand.

2.1 The Matching Principle

The matching precept states that prices need to be identified inside the identical length because of the sales they assist generate. In other words, expenses should be matched with the revenues they relate to, regardless of when the cash is received or paid. This principle ensures that financial statements accurately reflect the economic reality of the business's operations and performance.

For example, if a business sells products in January but doesn't receive payment until February, the revenue from the sale should be recognized in January, when the sale occurred, rather than in February when the cash is received. Similarly, expenses incurred in the process of generating revenue, such as cost of goods sold and operating expenses, should be recognized in the same period as the related revenue.

2.2 The Revenue Recognition Principle

The revenue recognition principle governs when and how revenue should be recognized in the financial statements. According to this principle, revenue should be recognized when it is earned and realizable, regardless of when cash is received. Revenue is considered earned when the business has fulfilled its obligations to the customer and is entitled to receive payment, and it is realizable when there is a reasonable expectation of collection.

For example, if a business provides services to a client in January but doesn't receive payment until February, the revenue from the services should be recognized in January, when the services were rendered, rather than in February when the payment is received. This ensures that revenue is recognized in the period in which it is earned, reflecting the economic value created by the business's operations.

2.3 The Principle of Conservatism

The principle of conservatism, also known as the principle of prudence, states that when faced with uncertainty or ambiguity, accountants should exercise caution and choose accounting methods and estimates that are least likely to overstate assets or income and understate liabilities or expenses. This principle helps ensure that financial statements are reliable, objective, and conservative in their presentation of the business's financial position and performance.

For example, if there is uncertainty about the collectability of accounts receivable, the principle of conservatism would require the business to recognize a provision for doubtful debts to account for the possibility of non-payment by customers. Similarly, if there is uncertainty about the value of inventory, the principle of conservatism would require the business to use the lower cost or market value to value inventory on the balance sheet.

2.4 The Principle of Materiality

The principle of materiality states that financial information should be presented and disclosed in a manner that is relevant, accurate, and meaningful to users, focusing on information that is material or significant. Materiality is assessed based on the impact that a misstatement or omission of financial information would have on the decisions of users, considering both quantitative and qualitative factors.

For example, if a business makes an error in recording a small transaction that has an immaterial impact on the financial statements, it may not be necessary to correct the error, as it would not affect the decisions of users. However, if the error has a material impact on the financial statements, it must be corrected to ensure the accuracy and reliability of the financial information presented to users.

Section 3: Setting Up Your Home Office for Success

Setting up a home office is an essential step in establishing and running a successful bookkeeping practice. In this section, we'll discuss practical tips and strategies for creating a productive and efficient home office environment that supports your business goals and maximizes your success.

3.1 Designing Your Workspace

Designate a dedicated space in your home for your bookkeeping practice, ideally a quiet and private area where you can focus and concentrate without distractions. Choose a comfortable and ergonomic workspace that promotes good posture and reduces fatigue and strain. Invest in quality office furniture, such as a desk, chair, and storage cabinets, that meets your needs and enhances your productivity and comfort.

Consider the layout and organization of your workspace to optimize efficiency and workflow. Arrange your desk and equipment in a way that minimizes clutter and maximizes accessibility to essential tools and resources.

Use storage solutions such as shelves, file cabinets, and bins to keep your office supplies, documents, and reference materials organized and easily accessible.

3.2 Equipping Your Office

Equip your home office with the necessary tools and equipment to support your bookkeeping activities and meet the needs of your clients. Invest in a reliable computer or laptop with sufficient processing power, memory, and storage capacity to run accounting software and handle large volumes of financial data. Choose accounting software that meets your needs and preferences, whether it's a cloud-based solution or a desktop application, and familiarize yourself with its features and functionalities.

Invest in a high-quality printer, scanner, and other peripherals to facilitate document management and communication with clients. Consider investing in ergonomic accessories such as a keyboard, mouse, and monitor to reduce strain and discomfort during long hours of work. Ensure that your home office is equipped with reliable internet access and communication tools such as email, phone, and video conferencing to stay connected with clients and colleagues.

3.3 Establishing Systems and Procedures

Establish systems and procedures to streamline your bookkeeping operations and ensure consistency and accuracy in your work. Develop standardized processes for recording and categorizing financial transactions, preparing financial statements, and communicating with clients. Create templates, checklists, and workflows to guide your work and minimize errors and oversights.

Implement file management systems and naming conventions to organize and store your digital files and documents efficiently. Create backup and data recovery procedures to protect your business data and ensure business continuity in the event of hardware failure, data loss, or security breaches. Establish security measures such as passwords, encryption, and access controls to safeguard sensitive financial information and protect client confidentiality.

3.4 Managing Your Time Effectively

Managing your time effectively is essential for maximizing productivity and achieving your business goals. Develop a daily routine and schedule that allows you to balance your bookkeeping responsibilities with other personal and professional commitments. Prioritize your tasks and allocate time for essential activities such as client meetings, data entry, reconciliation, and financial reporting.

Use time management techniques such as time blocking, prioritization, and delegation to optimize your productivity and focus on high-value activities that drive your business forward. Minimize distractions and interruptions during work hours by setting boundaries with family members, friends, and other distractions. Take regular breaks and recharge your energy and focus to maintain peak performance throughout the day.

In this Chapter, where we've laid the foundation for your success in the world of bookkeeping. Where we've explored the basics of bookkeeping, demystified essential accounting principles, and guided you in setting up your home office for maximum productivity and success.

As you continue on your journey, remember that mastering the fundamentals of bookkeeping is essential for building a strong and sustainable business. By understanding the basics of bookkeeping, embracing essential accounting principles, and creating a productive home office environment, you can lay the groundwork for success and excel in the dynamic and rewarding field of bookkeeping.

So take the knowledge and tools you've gained in this chapter and apply them to your practice as you strive to

achieve your goals and aspirations. Stay curious, keep learning, and never stop growing as you embark on this exciting journey towards financial fluency and success in the world of bookkeeping. The opportunities are endless, and the des
tiny is yours to create.

Chapter 2: Mastering Money Management

Welcome to the heart of financial success – mastering money management. In this comprehensive chapter, we delve into the essential skills and strategies for effectively managing income and expenses, creating budgets for your business and clients, and implementing profitable pricing strategies. From tracking every dollar that flows in and out of your business to setting prices that reflect the value you provide, we will guide you through the intricacies of money management and empower you to achieve financial prosperity.

Section 1: Tracking Income and Expenses Effectively

At the core of successful money management lies the ability to track every penny that enters and exits your business. In this section, we explore the importance of accurate and thorough income and expense tracking and provide practical tips and strategies for implementing effective tracking systems.

1.1 The Importance of Tracking Income and Expenses

Tracking income and expenses effectively is crucial for maintaining financial health and making informed business decisions. By monitoring your cash flow, you can identify trends, anticipate challenges, and seize growth opportunities. Additionally, accurate financial records are essential for tax compliance, budgeting, and financial reporting.

1.2 Establishing a Tracking System

To track income and expenses effectively, you need a reliable system in place. This system should be easy to use, scalable, and adaptable to your business's needs. Common tools for tracking income and expenses include accounting software, spreadsheets, and dedicated bookkeeping apps. Choose a system that aligns with your preferences and budget, and be sure to customize it to suit your business's unique requirements.

1.3 Categorizing Income and Expenses

Organizing your income and expenses into meaningful categories is essential for gaining insights into your financial performance. Common classes consist of revenue, value of products sold, working expenses, and taxes. Be consistent in your categorization and use clear labels to ensure accuracy and transparency.

1.4 Reconciling Financial Records

Regular reconciliation of your financial records is crucial for ensuring accuracy and identifying discrepancies.

Compare your records against bank statements, invoices, and receipts to verify the accuracy of your transactions. Address any discrepancies promptly and keep detailed records of your reconciliation efforts for future reference.

Section 2: Budgeting Techniques for Your Business and Clients

Budgeting is a critical component of financial planning and management, providing a roadmap for allocating resources and achieving financial goals. In this section, we explore the principles of budgeting and provide practical techniques for creating budgets for your business and clients.

2.1 Understanding the Importance of Budgeting

Budgeting helps businesses set goals, allocate resources, and track progress toward financial objectives. By establishing a budget, you can prioritize spending, identify areas for cost savings, and plan for future growth. Budgets also serve as a tool for communication and accountability, helping stakeholders understand financial expectations and responsibilities.

2.2 Types of Budgets

There are several types of budgets that businesses can use to manage their finances effectively. Common types include:

1. Operating Budgets: These budgets outline the expected revenue and expenses for a specific period, such as a fiscal year or quarter. Operating budgets help businesses plan for day-to-day operations and ensure that expenses do not exceed revenue.

2. Capital Budgets: Capital budgets focus on long-term investments, such as equipment purchases or facility upgrades. These budgets help businesses allocate funds for major projects and assess the potential return on investment.

3. Cash Flow Budgets: Cash flow budgets track the inflow and outflow of cash over a specific period. These budgets help businesses manage liquidity and ensure that they have enough cash on hand to meet their financial obligations.

2.3 Steps to Creating a Budget

Creating a budget involves several key steps:

1. Set Goals: Determine your financial objectives and establish clear, measurable goals for your budget.

2. Gather Data: Collect information about your income, expenses, and financial obligations. Use historical data, market research, and industry benchmarks to inform your budget projections.

3. Estimate Revenue: Forecast your expected revenue based on sales projections, pricing strategies, and market trends. Be realistic in your estimates and consider potential fluctuations in demand or economic conditions.

4. Identify Expenses: List all of your expenses, including fixed costs (e.g., rent, utilities) and variable costs (e.g., supplies, marketing). Be thorough in your assessment and consider both one-time and recurring expenses.

5. Allocate Resources: Allocate your resources based on your financial goals and priorities. Allocate funds to essential expenses first, such as payroll and overhead costs, before allocating funds to discretionary spending.

6. Monitor and Adjust: Regularly monitor your budget performance and compare actual results to budgeted projections. Adjust your price range as had to replicate modifications on your enterprise surroundings or monetary performance.

2.4 Budgeting for Clients

As a bookkeeper, you may also be responsible for creating budgets for your clients. When creating budgets for clients, it's essential to understand their financial goals, priorities, and constraints. Work closely with your clients to gather information about their income, expenses, and financial objectives, and develop a budget that aligns with their needs and expectations. Provide regular updates on budget performance and offer insights and recommendations for optimizing spending and achieving financial goals.

Section 3: Implementing Profitable Pricing Strategies

Setting prices that reflect the value you provide is essential for achieving profitability and sustainability in your bookkeeping business. In this section, we explore the principles of pricing and provide practical strategies for implementing profitable pricing strategies that maximize revenue and profit.

3.1 Understanding Pricing Principles

Effective pricing requires a deep understanding of your market, customers, and competition. Consider factors such as your costs, value proposition, and target market when setting prices. Pricing strategies should also reflect broader business objectives, such as revenue growth, market share, and brand positioning.

3.2 Factors to Consider When Pricing Services

When pricing bookkeeping services, consider the following factors:

1. Value: Price your services based on the value they provide to your clients. Consider the time and expertise required to deliver your services, as well as the potential cost savings and benefits to your clients.

2. Competition: Research your competitors' pricing strategies and benchmark your prices against industry standards. Differentiate your services based on quality, expertise, and customer service to justify higher prices.

3. Costs: Calculate your costs accurately to ensure that your prices cover expenses and generate a profit. Consider both direct costs (e.g., labor, materials) and indirect costs (e.g., overhead, utilities) when pricing your services.

3.3 Pricing Strategies

There are several pricing strategies that businesses can use to set prices effectively:

1. Cost-Plus Pricing: Set prices based on the cost of providing your services, plus a markup for profit. This approach ensures that your prices cover expenses and generate a desired profit margin.

2. Value-Based Pricing: Set prices based on the value your services provide to your clients. Focus on the benefits and outcomes your clients receive, rather than the cost of delivering your services.

3. Competitive Pricing: Set prices based on market conditions and competitors' pricing strategies. Price your services competitively to attract customers and differentiate your offerings based on quality and value.

3.4 Communicating Value to Clients

Communicating the value of your services is essential for justifying your prices and winning new clients. Focus on the benefits and outcomes your clients will receive, such as time savings, improved accuracy, and better financial decision-making. Use case studies, testimonials, and demonstrations to showcase your expertise and track record of success. Be transparent about your pricing and provide clear explanations for your rates to build trust and credibility with your clients.

Case Study: The Power of Profitable Pricing

To illustrate the importance of profitable pricing strategies, let's consider the case of Sarah, a freelance bookkeeper who recently launched her own business. Sarah offers a range of bookkeeping services to small businesses and entrepreneurs, including accounts payable, accounts receivable, payroll processing, and financial reporting.

When Sarah first started her business, she struggled to set prices that reflected the value she provided to her clients. She worried that if she set her prices too high, she would lose potential clients to competitors, but if she set her prices too low, she wouldn't be able to cover her costs and achieve profitability.

After conducting market research and analyzing her competitors' pricing strategies, Sarah realized that she was underestimating the value of her services and charging too little for her expertise and expertise. She decided to raise her prices to better reflect the value she provided and position herself as a premium provider of bookkeeping services.

To justify her new prices, Sarah communicated the benefits of her services to her clients, highlighting the time and money they would save by outsourcing their bookkeeping tasks to her. She also offered incentives such as discounts for long-term contracts and referral bonuses to encourage repeat business and word-of-mouth marketing.

The results were immediate and dramatic – Sarah's revenue increased significantly, and she attracted new clients who were willing to pay her higher prices for her quality services. By implementing profitable pricing strategies, Sarah was able to achieve her financial goals and build a thriving bookkeeping business that provided value to her clients and contributed to her long-term success and sustainability.

Congratulations! You've mastered the essentials of money management, from tracking income and expenses effectively to creating budgets for your business and clients and implementing profitable pricing strategies. Armed with these essential skills and strategies, you're well-equipped to achieve financial success and sustainability in your bookkeeping business.

By tracking your income and expenses effectively, creating and adhering to budgets, and setting prices that reflect the value you provide, you'll gain greater control over your finances, maximize revenue and profit, and achieve your long-term goals and aspirations. So take the first step towards financial prosperity today, and watch as your bookkeeping business thrives and grows beyond your wildest dreams.

Chapter 3: Digital Dynamo: Leveraging Technology for Efficiency

Welcome to the digital age of bookkeeping! In this dynamic chapter, we delve into the transformative power of technology in streamlining bookkeeping processes, boosting productivity, and enhancing security. From exploring the best bookkeeping software solutions to automating repetitive tasks and safeguarding client data, we will guide you through the digital landscape and empower you to become a digital dynamo in your bookkeeping practice.

Section 1: Exploring the Best Bookkeeping Software Solutions

In today's digital world, bookkeeping software solutions play a pivotal role in simplifying financial management tasks, organizing data, and providing valuable insights into business finances. In this section, we explore some of the top bookkeeping software solutions available on the market and discuss their features, benefits, and suitability for different business needs.

1.1 QuickBooks

QuickBooks is one of the most popular bookkeeping software solutions for small businesses and freelancers. It gives a huge variety of features, which include invoicing, fee tracking, payroll processing, and monetary reporting. QuickBooks is user-friendly and customizable, making it ideal for businesses of all sizes and industries. With its cloud-based platform, users can access their financial data anytime, anywhere, and collaborate with their accountant or bookkeeper in real time.

1.2 Xero

Xero is another leading bookkeeping software solution known for its simplicity, flexibility, and scalability. It gives complete capabilities for invoicing, financial institution reconciliation, rate tracking, and mission management. Xero's intuitive interface and robust reporting tools make it easy for users to manage their finances and make data-driven decisions. With its cloud-based platform, users can automate repetitive tasks, streamline workflows, and collaborate with their team in real time.

1.3 FreshBooks

FreshBooks is a cloud-based bookkeeping software solution designed specifically for freelancers and small service-based businesses. It offers features such as time tracking, expense management, invoicing, and project management. FreshBooks is known for its user-friendly interface and mobile app, making it easy for users to manage their finances on the go. With its automated features and integrations with other business tools, FreshBooks helps users save time, reduce errors, and focus on growing their business.

1.4 Wave

Wave is a free bookkeeping software solution that offers a range of features for small businesses and freelancers. It includes invoicing, expense tracking, accounting, and payroll processing tools. Wave is ideal for startups and small businesses with limited budgets, as it offers basic accounting functionality at no cost. With its easy-to-use interface and customizable features, Wave helps users stay organized, track their finances, and manage their business more efficiently.

1.5 Sage

Sage is a comprehensive bookkeeping software solution designed for small and medium-sized businesses. It offers features such as invoicing, expense tracking, inventory management, and financial reporting. Sage is known for its robust functionality and customizable features, making it suitable for businesses with complex accounting needs. With its cloud-based platform, users can access their financial data securely from any device, anywhere in the world.

Section 2: Automating Repetitive Tasks to Maximize Productivity

Automation is revolutionizing the way bookkeepers manage their tasks, saving time, reducing errors, and increasing efficiency. In this section, we explore some of the most common repetitive tasks in bookkeeping and discuss how automation can streamline these processes and boost productivity.

2.1 Data Entry

Data entry is one of the most time-consuming tasks in bookkeeping, requiring manual input of financial transactions into the accounting system. Automation tools such as optical character recognition (OCR) software can help streamline this process by scanning and extracting data from documents such as receipts, invoices, and bank statements. With OCR technology, bookkeepers can save time and reduce errors by automating the data entry process and importing financial information directly into their accounting software.

2.2 Bank Reconciliation

Bank reconciliation is another labor-intensive task in bookkeeping, requiring manual comparison of bank statements with accounting records to ensure accuracy and completeness. Automation tools such as bank feeds can simplify this process by automatically importing bank transactions into the accounting software and matching them with corresponding entries. With bank feeds, bookkeepers can reconcile accounts more quickly and accurately, identify discrepancies or errors, and detect fraudulent transactions in real time.

2.3 Invoicing and Billing

Invoicing and billing are essential tasks in bookkeeping, requiring timely and accurate generation of invoices and tracking of payments. Automation tools such as invoicing software can streamline this process by generating invoices automatically based on predefined templates and sending them to clients via email or other electronic channels. With invoicing software, bookkeepers can save time, reduce administrative overhead, and improve cash flow by expediting the billing process and facilitating prompt payment from clients.

2.4 Expense Management

Expense management is a critical aspect of bookkeeping, requiring careful tracking and categorization of business expenses for tax compliance and financial reporting purposes. Automation tools such as expense management software can simplify this process by allowing users to capture receipts digitally, categorize expenses automatically, and reconcile transactions with accounting records. With expense management software, bookkeepers can streamline expense tracking, ensure compliance with tax regulations, and gain insights into spending patterns and trends.

2.5 Reporting and Analysis

Reporting and analysis are essential tasks in bookkeeping, requiring the generation of financial reports and analysis of key performance indicators (KPIs) to assess business performance and inform strategic decision-making. Automation tools such as reporting software can streamline this process by generating customizable reports automatically based on predefined criteria and presenting data in visual formats such as charts and graphs. With reporting software, bookkeepers can save time, improve accuracy, and gain valuable insights into their business's financial health and performance.

Section 3: Securing Data and Protecting Client Confidentiality

In an increasingly digital world, data security and client confidentiality are paramount concerns for bookkeepers. In this section, we explore best practices for securing data and protecting client confidentiality in bookkeeping practices.

3.1 Data Encryption

Data encryption is a critical security measure for protecting sensitive financial information from unauthorized access or interception. Bookkeepers should encrypt data both in transit and at rest using strong encryption algorithms and secure communication protocols. Encryption ensures that data is securely transmitted and stored, reducing the risk of data breaches or unauthorized access.

3.2 Access Controls

Access controls help prevent unauthorized access to sensitive financial information by limiting access to authorized users only. Bookkeepers should implement strong password policies, multi-factor authentication, and role-based access controls to restrict access to sensitive data and systems. Access controls ensure that only authorized personnel can view, edit, or delete financial information, reducing the risk of data breaches or insider threats.

3.3 Data Backups

Data backups are essential for protecting against data loss due to hardware failure, human error, or cyber-attacks. Bookkeepers should implement regular backups of their accounting data to secure off-site locations or cloud storage providers. Backup solutions should be automated, encrypted, and regularly tested to ensure data integrity and availability in the event of a disaster or security incident.

3.4 Data Privacy

Data privacy is a legal requirement for bookkeepers handling sensitive financial information, such as the personal and financial data of clients. Bookkeepers should comply with data protection regulations such as the General Data Protection Regulation (GDPR) and implement policies and procedures to safeguard client confidentiality and privacy. Data privacy measures should include obtaining consent for data processing, securely storing and disposing of data, and notifying clients of any data breaches or security incidents.

3.5 Cybersecurity

Cybersecurity is a growing concern for bookkeepers due to the increasing frequency and sophistication of cyber attacks targeting financial data. Bookkeepers should implement cybersecurity measures such as firewalls, antivirus software, and intrusion detection systems to protect against malware, phishing, and other cyber threats. Regular security audits and penetration testing can help identify vulnerabilities and weaknesses in the bookkeeping system and mitigate the risk of security breaches.

Congratulations! You've unlocked the power of technology in bookkeeping, from exploring the best bookkeeping software solutions to automating repetitive tasks, securing data, and protecting client confidentiality. Armed with these digital tools and strategies, you're well-equipped to maximize efficiency, productivity, and security in your bookkeeping practice.

By leveraging technology effectively, you can streamline bookkeeping processes, reduce manual effort, and focus on delivering value-added services to your clients. So embrace the digital revolution in bookkeeping, and watch as your practice thrives and grows in the digital age.

Chapter 4: Building Your Brand and Client Base

Welcome to the world of brand building and client acquisition! In this transformative chapter, we'll dive deep into the art of crafting a compelling brand identity, implementing effective marketing strategies to attract ideal clients, and nurturing long-term relationships for referrals and repeat business. By the end of this chapter, you'll be well-equipped to establish a strong brand presence, attract your dream clients, and cultivate lasting relationships that fuel the growth of your bookkeeping business.

Section 1: Crafting a Compelling Brand Identity

Your brand identity is the foundation of your bookkeeping business – it's what sets you apart from the competition and communicates your unique value proposition to potential clients. In this section, we'll explore the key elements of crafting a compelling brand identity that resonates with your target audience and leaves a lasting impression.

1.1 Defining Your Brand

The first step in crafting a compelling brand identity is defining what your brand stands for and what sets it apart from competitors. Start by identifying your core values, mission, and vision for your bookkeeping business. What do you want to achieve, and what principles will guide your actions? Define your brand personality – is it professional, approachable, trustworthy, or innovative? Understanding your brand's essence will help you communicate it effectively to your target audience.

1.2 Creating Your Brand Assets

Once you've defined your brand, it's time to bring it to life through visual and verbal elements. Develop a logo, color palette, and typography that reflect your brand's personality and resonate with your target audience. Your logo property needs to be regular throughout all advertising materials, together with your website, enterprise cards, and social media profiles. Create a brand style guide to ensure consistency in messaging and design across all touchpoints.

1.3 Crafting Your Brand Story

Every brand has a story – it's what connects you with your audience on a deeper level and sets the stage for building meaningful relationships. Craft a compelling emblem tale that communicates who you are, what you do, and why you do it. Share your journey, your passion for bookkeeping, and the value you bring to your clients. Your brand story should be authentic, relatable, and memorable, leaving a lasting impression on your audience.

1.4 Building Your Online Presence

In today's digital world, your online presence is often the first impression potential clients have of your brand. Invest in a professional website that showcases your brand identity, services, and testimonials from satisfied clients. Optimize your website for search engines to improve visibility and attract organic traffic. Establish a presence on social media platforms such as LinkedIn, Facebook, and Instagram to engage with your audience and share valuable content.

Section 2: Marketing Strategies to Attract Ideal Clients

With a compelling brand identity in place, it's time to attract your dream clients and grow your bookkeeping business. In this section, we'll explore effective marketing strategies to reach your target audience, generate leads, and convert prospects into paying clients.

2.1 Identifying Your Ideal Client

Before you can market your services effectively, you need to understand who your ideal client is and what they need. Conduct marketplace studies to pick out your goal audience's demographics, preferences, and ache points. What industries do they belong to? What challenges are they facing in their bookkeeping needs? Tailor your marketing efforts to address their specific needs and position yourself as the solution to their problems.

2.2 Content Marketing

Content marketing is a powerful strategy for attracting and engaging your target audience by providing valuable, relevant content that addresses their pain points and interests. Create blog posts, articles, videos, and infographics that showcase your expertise and provide insights into common bookkeeping challenges. Share your content on your website, social media channels, and email newsletters to establish yourself as a thought leader and attract potential clients.

2.3 Networking and Relationship Building

Networking is a valuable tool for building connections, establishing credibility, and generating referrals for your bookkeeping business. Attend industry events, join professional associations, and participate in networking groups to meet potential clients and referral partners. Build relationships with fellow professionals, business owners, and influencers in your niche, and leverage these connections to expand your client base and grow your business through word-of-mouth marketing.

2.4 Digital Advertising

Digital advertising allows you to reach your target audience quickly and efficiently through platforms such as Google Ads, Facebook Ads, and LinkedIn Ads. Develop targeted ad campaigns that speak directly to your ideal client's needs and pain points, and use demographic and interest targeting to reach them where they spend time online. Monitor your ad performance regularly and adjust your targeting and messaging based on feedback to optimize your results and maximize your return on investment.

2.5 Referral Marketing

Referral marketing is one of the most effective ways to attract new clients to your bookkeeping business. Encourage satisfied clients to refer their friends, family, and colleagues to your services by offering incentives such as discounts, bonuses, or free consultations. Build a referral program that rewards clients for referring new business and makes it easy for them to spread the word about your services. Cultivate relationships with referral partners
 such as accountants, lawyers, and business consultants who can refer clients to you in exchange for a commission or reciprocal referrals.

Section 3: Nurturing Long-Term Relationships for Referrals and Repeat Business

While attracting new clients is essential for growing your bookkeeping business, nurturing long-term relationships with existing clients is equally important. In this section, we'll explore strategies for fostering loyalty, generating referrals, and encouraging repeat business from satisfied clients.

3.1 Providing Exceptional Service

The basis of any hit patron dating is amazing service. Go above and beyond to exceed your client's expectations and deliver results that wow them. Be responsive to their needs, proactive in addressing their concerns, and attentive to their feedback. By providing exceptional service, you'll build trust, loyalty, and goodwill with your clients, laying the groundwork for long-term relationships and repeat business.

3.2 Communication and Transparency

Effective communication is essential for maintaining strong client relationships and keeping them informed and engaged. Keep lines of communication open with your clients through regular check-ins, updates, and status reports. Be transparent about your processes, pricing, and expectations to avoid misunderstandings or conflicts. Listen to your clients' feedback and address any concerns or issues promptly to demonstrate your commitment to their satisfaction.

3.3 Adding Value

Find ways to add value to your client relationships beyond your core bookkeeping services. Offer additional services such as financial planning, tax preparation, or business consulting to help your clients achieve their goals and overcome challenges. Share relevant resources, insights, and industry trends that can help your clients make informed decisions and stay ahead of the curve. By adding value to your client relationships, you'll position yourself as a trusted advisor and partner in their success.

3.4 Asking for Feedback and Reviews

Feedback is a valuable tool for improving your services and strengthening your client relationships. Regularly solicit feedback from your clients through surveys, reviews, or one-on-one conversations to gauge their satisfaction and identify areas for improvement. Act on feedback promptly and make adjustments to your processes or services as needed to address any concerns or issues. Encourage satisfied clients to leave positive reviews and testimonials on your website, social media, or review platforms to attract new clients and build credibility.

3.5 Cultivating Referral Relationships

Referral relationships are a powerful source of new business for your bookkeeping practice. Nurture relationships with existing clients, referral partners, and industry contacts who can refer clients to you in exchange for a commission or reciprocal referrals. Keep these relationships top of mind by staying in touch regularly, providing updates on your services and offerings, and offering incentives for referrals. By cultivating referral relationships, you'll tap into a steady stream of high-quality leads and grow your client base organically.

Congratulations! You've unlocked the secrets to building a strong brand presence and client base for your bookkeeping business. By crafting a compelling brand identity, implementing effective marketing strategies, and nurturing long-term relationships, you'll attract your dream clients, foster loyalty, and fuel the growth of your business.

So go forth and build your brand, attract your ideal clients, and cultivate lasting relationships that propel your bookkeeping business to new heights. With the right strategies and mindset, the sky's the limit for your success in the world of bookkeeping.

Chapter 5: From Keyboard to Cash: Managing Cash Flow Like a Pro

Welcome to the realm of cash flow management, where the mastery of financial liquidity can spell the difference between success and struggle. In this enlightening chapter, we'll delve into the art and science of optimizing cash flow for your bookkeeping business and clients, navigating common challenges, and implementing strategies for sustainable growth and expansion. So buckle up and get ready to unlock the secrets to managing cash flow like a seasoned pro.

Section 1: Optimizing Cash Flow for Your Business and Clients

Cash goes with the drift is the lifeblood of any business – it is what maintains the lighting on, the payments paid, and the operations strolling smoothly. In this section, we'll explore strategies for optimizing cash flow for your bookkeeping business and clients, ensuring financial stability and success.

1.1 Understanding Cash Flow

Before we can optimize cash flow, it's essential to understand what it is and how it works. Cash flow refers to the movement of money in and out of a business over a specific period, typically measured monthly, quarterly, or annually. Positive cash flow occurs when the money coming into the business exceeds the money going out, while negative cash flow occurs when expenses exceed revenue. Understanding your cash flow cycle and identifying key drivers of cash flow can help you make informed decisions and manage your finances effectively.

1.2 Cash Flow Forecasting

Cash flow forecasting is a crucial tool for predicting future cash flow trends and identifying potential cash shortages or surpluses. By analyzing historical data, market trends, and upcoming expenses and revenue, you can create a cash flow forecast that helps you anticipate cash flow fluctuations and plan accordingly. Regularly review and update your cash flow forecast to reflect changes in your business environment and ensure accuracy in your projections.

1.3 Managing Accounts Receivable

Accounts receivable management is essential for maintaining positive cash flow and ensuring timely payment from clients. Implement clear invoicing procedures, including detailed invoices with payment terms and deadlines. Follow up promptly on overdue invoices and establish a system for tracking payment status and communicating with clients about outstanding balances. Consider offering incentives for early payment or penalties for late payment to encourage timely payment and improve cash flow.

1.4 Controlling Accounts Payable

Accounts payable management is equally important for managing cash flow and maintaining financial stability. Negotiate favorable payment terms with suppliers and vendors, including discounts for early payment or extended payment terms. Prioritize payments based on due dates and cash availability, and consider leveraging payment solutions such as business credit cards or lines of credit to manage cash flow gaps or unexpected expenses.

1.5 Managing Inventory and Expenses

Effective inventory and expense management are critical for optimizing cash flow and reducing costs. Monitor inventory levels closely and implement inventory management systems to track inventory turnover, minimize carrying costs, and avoid stock outs or overstock situations. Review expenses regularly and identify opportunities for cost savings or efficiency improvements, such as renegotiating contracts, reducing discretionary spending, or consolidating suppliers.

Section 2: Overcoming Common Cash Flow Challenges

Despite your best efforts, cash flow challenges are inevitable in the course of running a bookkeeping business. In this section, we'll explore common cash flow challenges faced by bookkeepers and clients alike and discuss strategies for overcoming them.

2.1 Seasonal Fluctuations

Seasonal fluctuations in revenue and expenses can wreak havoc on cash flow, causing cash shortages or surpluses at different times of the year. To mitigate the impact of seasonal fluctuations, create a cash flow forecast that takes into account seasonal trends and plan accordingly. Build up cash reserves during peak seasons to cover expenses during slow periods, and adjust your marketing and pricing strategies to smooth out revenue streams throughout the year.

2.2 Late Payments and Bad Debts

Late payments and bad debts are a common headache for bookkeepers, leading to cash flow disruptions and financial losses. To address late payments, implement clear invoicing procedures, including detailed invoices with payment terms and deadlines. Follow up promptly on overdue invoices and establish a system for tracking payment status and communicating with clients about outstanding balances. Consider offering incentives for early payment or penalties for late payment to encourage timely payment and reduce the risk of bad debts.

2.3 Unexpected Expenses

Unexpected expenses can arise at any time, from equipment breakdowns to legal disputes, posing a significant challenge to cash flow management. To prepare for unexpected expenses, build up an emergency fund or reserve account to cover unforeseen costs without disrupting cash flow. Consider purchasing insurance coverage or warranties to protect against major risks and liabilities and implement risk management strategies to identify and mitigate potential threats to your business.

2.4 Economic Downturns

Economic downturns can have a profound impact on cash flow, causing revenue declines, increased competition, and reduced consumer spending. To weather economic downturns, focus on building strong client relationships, diversifying your client base, and offering value-added services that address clients' changing needs and priorities. Reduce discretionary spending, conserve cash during lean times, and invest in marketing and business development initiatives to position your business for growth when economic conditions improve.

Section 3: Strategies for Growth and Expansion

Cash flow management is not just about survival – it's also about fueling growth and expansion. In this section, we'll explore strategies for leveraging cash flow to drive business growth and expand your bookkeeping practice.

3.1 Investing in Marketing and Business Development

Investing in marketing and business development initiatives is essential for attracting new clients, expanding your client base, and growing your bookkeeping practice. Allocate a portion of your cash flow to marketing activities such as advertising, social media, and content marketing to increase visibility and generate leads. Invest in networking events, industry conferences, and professional development opportunities to build relationships with potential clients and referral partners and position yourself as a trusted advisor and expert in your field.

3.2 Expanding Service Offerings

Expanding your service offerings is another strategy for leveraging cash flow to drive business growth and diversify your revenue streams. Consider offering value-added services such as tax preparation, financial planning, or business consulting to meet clients' evolving needs and increase your value proposition. Invest in training and certification programs to develop expertise in new service areas and differentiate yourself from competitors. By expanding your service offerings, you can attract new clients, increase client retention, and generate additional revenue for your bookkeeping practice.

3.3 Investing in Technology and Infrastructure

Investing in technology and infrastructure is essential for improving efficiency, scalability, and competitiveness in the bookkeeping industry. Allocate funds to upgrade your accounting software, hardware, and IT infrastructure to streamline processes, automate repetitive tasks, and enhance data security. Invest in training and education for yourself and your team to stay abreast of the latest technological developments and best practices in bookkeeping. By investing in technology and infrastructure, you can position your business for long-term success and growth in an increasingly digital world.

3.4 Acquiring or Merging with Other Firms

Acquiring or merging with other bookkeeping firms can be a strategic way to grow your business and expand your client base. Look for firms that complement your strengths, fill gaps in your service offerings, or operate in complementary geographic markets. Conduct due diligence to assess the financial health, client base, and culture fit of potential acquisition targets or merger partners. Negotiate terms that are favorable to both parties and ensure a smooth transition for clients and employees. By acquiring or merging with other firms, you can achieve economies of scale, increase market share, and position your business for accelerated growth and success.

Congratulations! You've mastered the art and science of managing cash flow like a pro, from optimizing cash flow for your bookkeeping business and clients to overcoming common challenges and implementing strategies for growth and expansion. By leveraging cash flow effectively, you can ensure financial stability, fuel business growth, and achieve your long-term goals and aspirations in the world of bookkeeping.

So take control of your cash flow, seize opportunities for growth and expansion, and watch as your bookkeeping practice flourishes and thrives in the years to come. With the right strategies and mindset, the sky's the limit for your success in managing cash flow like a seasoned pro.

Chapter 6: Scaling Your Success: Going from Solo to Small Team

Welcome to the exciting journey of scaling your bookkeeping business from a one-person operation to a small team. In this chapter, we'll explore the intricacies of hiring and training assistants or employees, delegating tasks to maintain efficiency, and managing growth while ensuring quality service. Whether you're expanding to meet growing demand or simply looking to increase productivity and capacity, this chapter will guide you through the process of building and managing a successful team.

Section 1: Hiring and Training Assistants or Employees

Expanding your bookkeeping business to include a small team is an important milestone that can unlock new opportunities for growth and success. However, it's essential to approach hiring and training with careful planning and consideration to ensure that you build a cohesive and effective team. In this section, we'll explore best practices for hiring and training assistants or employees to support your business's growth and expansion.

1.1 Defining Roles and Responsibilities

Before you can hire assistants or employees, it's crucial to define the roles and responsibilities you need to fill within your team. Start by assessing your business's needs, identifying areas where additional support is needed, and defining the specific tasks and duties associated with each role. Consider factors such as technical skills, experience level, and cultural fit when determining the qualifications and requirements for each position.

1.2 Crafting Job Descriptions

Once you've defined the roles and responsibilities for your team, it's time to craft detailed job descriptions that accurately reflect the requirements and expectations for each position. Clearly outline the duties, responsibilities, and qualifications for the role, including required skills, experience, and education. Be transparent about compensation, benefits, and opportunities for growth and advancement to attract qualified candidates and set clear expectations from the outset.

1.3 Recruiting and Hiring

Recruiting and hiring the right candidates is critical to building a successful team that can support your business's growth and expansion. Develop a comprehensive recruitment strategy that includes sourcing candidates through multiple channels, such as job boards, professional networks, and referrals. Screen candidates carefully to assess their qualifications, skills, and cultural fit, and conduct thorough interviews to evaluate their suitability for the role. Select candidates who align with your business's values, vision, and goals, and who demonstrate the potential to contribute to your team's success.

1.4 Onboarding and Training

Once you've hired assistants or employees, it's essential to onboard and train them effectively to ensure a smooth transition and set them up for success in their roles. Develop a structured onboarding process that introduces new hires to your business, culture, and team dynamics, and provides them with the information and resources they need to hit the ground running. Provide comprehensive training on your business processes, systems, and tools, and offer ongoing support and guidance to help new hires acclimate to their roles and responsibilities. By investing in effective onboarding and training, you can empower your team members to perform at their best and contribute to your business's success from day one.

Section 2: Delegating Tasks to Maintain Efficiency

As your bookkeeping business grows and expands, it's essential to delegate tasks effectively to maintain efficiency and productivity. Delegating tasks allows you to focus on high-priority activities and strategic initiatives while empowering your team members to take on greater responsibility and contribute to the business's success. In this section, we'll explore strategies for delegating tasks to maintain efficiency and optimize your team's performance.

2.1 Identifying Tasks for Delegation

The first step in effective delegation is identifying tasks that can be delegated to your team members. Start by assessing your workload and identifying tasks that are time-consuming, repetitive, or outside your area of expertise. Consider your team members' skills, experience, and availability when determining which tasks are suitable for delegation and match them with appropriate responsibilities that align with their strengths and interests.

2.2 Setting Clear Expectations

Once you've identified tasks for delegation, it's crucial to set clear expectations and guidelines for how they should be completed. Communicate the scope of work, deadlines, and quality standards for each task, and provide any necessary instructions, resources, or support to help your team members succeed. Be available to answer questions, provide feedback, and address any challenges or concerns that arise during the delegation process, and ensure that your team members feel empowered and supported in their roles.

2.3 Empowering Team Members

Delegating tasks is not just about assigning work – it's also about empowering your team members to take ownership of their responsibilities and contribute to the business's success. Encourage autonomy and initiative by giving your team members the freedom to make decisions, solve problems, and innovate in their roles. Provide opportunities for growth and development, such as training, mentorship, and career advancement, to help your team members reach their full potential and continue to excel in their roles.

2.4 Monitoring Progress and Providing Feedback

Effective delegation requires ongoing monitoring of progress and performance to ensure that tasks are completed satisfactorily and on time. Establish regular check-ins, progress updates, and performance reviews to monitor your team members' progress, provide feedback on their work, and address any issues or concerns that arise. Recognize and celebrate achievements and milestones to motivate and inspire your team members to continue performing at their best, and be proactive in addressing any challenges or obstacles that may impede their progress.

Section 3: Managing Growth and Ensuring Quality Service

As your bookkeeping business continues to grow and expand, it's essential to manage growth effectively while maintaining the quality of service that your clients expect and deserve. In this section, we'll explore strategies for managing growth and ensuring quality service as you scale your team and expand your business operations.

3.1 Scaling Operations

Scaling your bookkeeping business requires careful planning and execution to ensure that your operations can support increased demand and capacity. Invest in scalable systems, processes, and infrastructure that can accommodate growth and expansion without sacrificing efficiency or quality. Automate repetitive tasks, streamline workflows, and leverage technology to optimize productivity and minimize errors. Continuously evaluate and adjust your operations to meet evolving client needs and market demands and ensure that your business remains agile and adaptable in the face of change.

3.2 Maintaining Quality Service

Maintaining quality service is paramount to sustaining client satisfaction and loyalty as your business grows and expands. Prioritize client communication, responsiveness, and transparency to foster trust and confidence in your services. Set and consistently meet high standards for accuracy, reliability, and professionalism in your work, and strive to exceed client expectations at every opportunity. Monitor client feedback and satisfaction levels regularly and take proactive measures to address any issues or concerns that arise. By prioritizing quality service, you can build a strong reputation, attract new clients through word-of-mouth referrals, and position your business for long-term success and growth.

3.3 Developing a Strong Company Culture

As your team grows and evolves, it's essential to cultivate a strong company culture that aligns with your business values, vision, and goals. Foster a supportive, inclusive, and collaborative work environment where team members feel valued, respected, and empowered to contribute their ideas and perspectives. Encourage open communication, teamwork, and camaraderie among your team members, and celebrate achievements and milestones together. Lead by example embodies the values and principles that you want to instill in your team, and foster a culture of continuous learning, growth, and innovation that drives excellence and success in your bookkeeping business.

3.4 Managing Change and Adaptation

As your bookkeeping business evolves and grows, you'll inevitably encounter changes and challenges along the way. Whether it's changes in client needs, market conditions, or industry trends, it's essential to remain flexible, adaptable, and resilient in the face of change. Embrace change as an opportunity for growth and innovation, and approach challenges with a positive attitude and a willingness to learn and evolve. Communicate openly and transparently with your team members about changes and their implications, and involve them in the decision-making process to foster buy-in and alignment. By effectively managing change and adaptation, you can navigate uncertainty and complexity with confidence and position your business for continued success and sustainability in the long term.

Congratulations! You've embarked on the journey of scaling your bookkeeping business from a solo operation to a small team, equipped with the knowledge, strategies, and mindset to succeed. By hiring and training assistants or employees effectively, delegating tasks to maintain efficiency, and managing growth while ensuring quality service, you can build a successful and sustainable bookkeeping practice that delivers exceptional value to your clients and drives long-term success and growth.

So embrace the challenge of scaling your success, and let your passion, vision, and determination guide you as you build and lead a high-performing team that propels your bookkeeping business to new heights. With the right approach and commitment to excellence, the possibilities are endless for your success in the world of bookkeeping.

Chapter 7: Navigating Legal and Compliance Waters

Welcome to Chapter 7 of your book, where we dive into the critical aspects of navigating legal and compliance requirements for your bookkeeping business. In this chapter, we will explore the intricacies of understanding tax obligations for both your business and clients, ensuring compliance with regulations and standards, and building a robust legal foundation to safeguard your bookkeeping practice.

Section 1: Understanding Tax Obligations for Your Business and Clients

Tax compliance is a cornerstone of responsible business ownership, and as a bookkeeper, you play a pivotal role in helping your clients meet their tax obligations. However, it's equally important to ensure that your own business adheres to tax laws and regulations. In this section, we'll delve into the complexities of understanding tax obligations for your business and clients, and how to navigate them effectively.

1.1 Tax Obligations for Your Business

As a business owner, you are responsible for fulfilling various tax obligations at the local, state, and federal levels. These may include income taxes, payroll taxes, sales taxes, and more, depending on the nature of your business and its operations. It's essential to understand the specific tax requirements that apply to your business and ensure compliance to avoid penalties, fines, or legal issues.

1.2 Tax Obligations for Your Clients

In addition to managing your tax obligations, you must also assist your clients in meeting their tax obligations. This may involve preparing and filing tax returns, calculating tax liabilities, and ensuring compliance with tax laws and regulations. As a trusted advisor, it's crucial to stay updated on changes to tax laws and regulations that may impact your clients and provide guidance and support to help them navigate complex tax matters effectively.

1.3 Tax Planning and Strategies

Tax planning is a proactive approach to managing your tax obligations and optimizing your tax position. By carefully planning and strategizing, you can minimize tax liabilities, maximize deductions and credits, and optimize your tax efficiency. Work closely with your clients to develop tax planning strategies tailored to their specific needs and circumstances, and help them implement strategies to minimize tax exposure and maximize tax savings.

1.4 Record Keeping and Documentation

Effective record-keeping and documentation are essential for ensuring compliance with tax laws and regulations. Maintain accurate and detailed records of income, expenses, deductions, and credits for both your business and your clients. Keep copies of all relevant documents, such as invoices, receipts, bank statements, and tax returns, organized and easily accessible for reference and audit purposes. Implement robust accounting systems and software to streamline record-keeping processes and ensure the accuracy and completeness of financial data.

Section 2: Compliance with Regulations and Standards

Compliance with regulations and standards is critical for maintaining the integrity and credibility of your bookkeeping practice. In this section, we'll explore the various regulatory and industry standards that govern the bookkeeping profession and discuss strategies for ensuring compliance and upholding ethical standards.

2.1 Regulatory Compliance

As a bookkeeper, you are subject to various regulatory requirements that govern the accounting and bookkeeping profession. These may include licensing, registration, and certification requirements, as well as compliance with laws and regulations related to data privacy, confidentiality, and ethics. Stay informed about regulatory developments and changes that may impact your practice, and ensure that you comply with all applicable regulations to avoid legal and reputational risks.

2.2 Professional Standards and Ethics

Maintaining high professional standards and ethics is essential for earning the trust and confidence of your clients and colleagues. Adhere to the principles of integrity, objectivity, competence, and confidentiality in all aspects of your practice, and uphold the ethical standards set forth by professional organizations and regulatory bodies. Avoid conflicts of interest, maintain independence and impartiality in your work, and always act in the best interests of your clients and the public trust.

2.3 Data Privacy and Confidentiality

Data privacy and confidentiality are paramount in the bookkeeping profession, given the sensitive nature of financial information. Safeguard client data and confidential information from unauthorized access, disclosure, or misuse, and implement robust security measures to protect against data breaches and cyber threats. Adhere to industry best practices and standards for data privacy and security, and ensure compliance with relevant laws and regulations, such as the General Data Protection Regulation (GDPR) and The Health Insurance Portability and Accountability Act (HIPAA).

2.4 Anti-Money Laundering and Fraud Prevention

Anti-money laundering (AML) and fraud prevention are critical priorities for bookkeepers, as they play a key role in detecting and deterring financial crime. Implement robust AML and fraud prevention policies and procedures to identify suspicious activities, report suspicious transactions to appropriate authorities, and mitigate the risk of money laundering, fraud, and financial crime. Stay vigilant to signs of fraudulent behavior, and take prompt action to investigate and address any concerns or suspicions.

Section 3: Building a Strong Legal Foundation for Your Bookkeeping Business

Building a strong legal foundation is essential for protecting your bookkeeping business from legal risks and liabilities. In this section, we'll explore the key legal considerations and strategies for establishing and maintaining a legally compliant and resilient bookkeeping practice.

3.1 Business Structure and Registration

Choosing the right business structure is a crucial decision that can impact your legal and tax obligations, as well as your liability. Consider factors such as liability protection, tax treatment, and administrative requirements when selecting a business structure, such as a sole proprietorship, partnership, corporation, or limited liability company (LLC). Register your business with the appropriate state and local authorities and obtain any necessary licenses or permits to operate legally in your jurisdiction.

3.2 Contracts and Agreements

Contracts and agreements are essential legal documents that govern the terms and conditions of your relationships with clients, vendors, employees, and other parties. Draft clear, comprehensive contracts and agreements that outline the rights, responsibilities, and obligations of all parties involved, including the scope of services, payment terms, confidentiality provisions, and dispute resolution mechanisms. Review contracts carefully before signing and seek legal advice if needed to ensure that your interests are protected and your rights are upheld.

3.3 Insurance Coverage

Insurance coverage is an essential safeguard for protecting your bookkeeping business from unexpected risks and liabilities. Obtain appropriate insurance coverage, such as professional liability insurance, general liability insurance, and cyber liability insurance, to mitigate the financial impact of potential lawsuits, claims, or damages. Review your insurance policies regularly to ensure that they provide adequate coverage for your business's needs and update them as necessary to reflect changes in your operations or risk profile.

3.4 Compliance with Employment Laws

If you have employees or plan to hire staff, compliance with employment laws and regulations is essential to ensure fair and lawful treatment of your employees and maintain a positive work environment. Familiarize yourself with federal, state, and local employment laws that govern areas such as wages, hours, overtime, workplace safety, and discrimination, and ensure that your policies and practices comply with all applicable legal requirements. Implement fair employment practices, provide clear policies and procedures, and address any concerns or complaints from employees promptly and effectively to foster a supportive and compliant workplace culture.

Congratulations! You've successfully navigated the legal and compliance waters of the bookkeeping profession, armed with the knowledge, strategies, and tools to ensure legal compliance, ethical conduct, and professional excellence in your practice. By understanding tax obligations for your business and clients, complying with regulations and standards, and building a strong legal foundation, you can protect your business from legal risks and liabilities and uphold the highest standards of integrity and professionalism in your work.

So continue to prioritize legal compliance, ethical conduct, and professional excellence in your bookkeeping practice, and let your commitment to integrity and compliance guide you as you navigate the complexities of the legal and regulatory landscape. With the right approach and mindset, you can build a successful and sustainable bookkeeping business that stands the test of time and earns the trust and confidence of your clients and stakeholders.

Chapter 8: Beyond Bookkeeping: Diversifying Your Revenue Streams

Welcome to Chapter 8 of your book, where we explore the exciting realm of diversifying your revenue streams beyond traditional bookkeeping services. In this chapter, we'll delve into the possibilities of offering additional services to your clients, creating passive income opportunities, and expanding your business horizons to unlock new sources of revenue and growth. So let's embark on this adventure of exploration and discovery together.

Section 1: Exploring Additional Services to Offer Clients

As a bookkeeper, you possess a unique skill set and expertise that can be leveraged to offer a wide range of additional services to your clients. In this section, we'll explore some of the most popular and lucrative additional services that you can offer to expand your service offerings and meet the diverse needs of your clients.

1.1 Financial Consulting and Advisory Services

One of the most natural extensions of bookkeeping services is offering financial consulting and advisory services to your clients. Use your expertise in financial management, budgeting, and forecasting to provide strategic guidance and advice to help your clients make informed decisions and achieve their financial goals. Offer services such as financial analysis, cash flow management, investment advisory, and strategic planning to add value and differentiate your practice in the marketplace.

1.2 Tax Preparation and Planning

Tax preparation and planning are natural complements to bookkeeping services, as they go hand in hand in managing your client's financial affairs. Expand your services to include tax preparation, filing, and planning to help your clients navigate complex tax laws and regulations, minimize tax liabilities, and maximize tax savings. Stay updated on changes to tax laws and regulations and provide proactive tax planning advice to help your clients stay compliant and optimize their tax position.

1.3 Payroll Services

Payroll processing is a time-consuming and complex task for many small businesses, making it an attractive service offering for bookkeepers. Expand your services to include payroll processing, tax withholding, and compliance to help your clients streamline their payroll operations and ensure accuracy and compliance with payroll laws and regulations. Offer additional services such as direct deposit, employee benefits administration, and payroll tax reporting to provide comprehensive payroll solutions to your clients.

1.4 Business Planning and Strategy

Help your clients plan and strategize for success by offering business planning and strategy services. Use your financial expertise to help clients develop business plans, set goals, and create strategies to achieve growth and profitability. Offer services such as market research, competitive analysis, feasibility studies, and business modeling to help clients make informed decisions and navigate challenges and opportunities in their industries.

1.5 Virtual CFO Services

Many small businesses lack the resources to hire a full-time chief financial officer (CFO), making virtual CFO services an attractive option for outsourcing financial management and strategy. Position yourself as a virtual

CFO and offer services such as financial reporting, budgeting, forecasting, and financial analysis to provide high-level financial expertise and strategic guidance to your clients. Serve as a trusted advisor and partner in your client's success by helping them make sound financial decisions and achieve their business objectives.

Section 2: Creating Passive Income Opportunities

Passive profits are the holy grail of monetary independence, permitting you to earn cash with minimum attempt or lively involvement. In this section, we'll explore some creative ways to create passive income opportunities using your bookkeeping skills and expertise.

2.1 Online Courses and Training

Share your knowledge and expertise with others by creating online courses and training programs on bookkeeping and financial management topics. Develop high-quality educational content, such as video tutorials, webinars, and e-books, and sell them through online platforms such as Udemy, Teachable, or your website. Monetize your expertise and generate passive income by offering valuable resources and training to individuals and businesses seeking to improve their financial literacy and skills.

2.2 Affiliate Marketing

Affiliate advertising is a famous passive earnings method that entails selling services or products and receiving a fee for every sale or referral. Partner with companies that offer products or services related to bookkeeping, accounting software, or financial management tools, and promote them to your audience through your website, blog, or social media channels. Earn passive income by referring clients or customers to these companies and receiving a commission for each sale or referral generated through your affiliate links.

2.3 Royalties and Licensing

If you've authored books, created software, or developed proprietary tools or resources related to bookkeeping or financial management, consider licensing or selling the rights to your intellectual property to earn royalties. License your content, software, or tools to other businesses, publishers, or organizations in exchange for a licensing fee or royalty payments based on usage or sales. Generate passive income by leveraging your intellectual property and earning royalties from ongoing sales or usage.

2.4 Rental Income

If you own commercial real estate or office space, consider renting out space to other businesses or professionals in related industries. Offer shared office space, coworking desks, or meeting rooms to bookkeepers, accountants, or small businesses looking for affordable workspace. Generate passive income from rental payments and leverage your real estate assets to diversify your income streams and build wealth over time.

Section 3: Expanding Your Business Horizons

As a bookkeeper, you have the opportunity to expand your business horizons and explore new avenues for growth and success. In this section, we'll discuss strategies for expanding your business beyond traditional bookkeeping services and seizing opportunities for innovation and entrepreneurship.

3.1 Specialization and Niche Markets

Differentiate yourself from competitors and carve out a unique position in the market by specializing in a specific niche or industry. Focus on serving niche markets such as healthcare, real estate, or e-commerce, where you have specialized knowledge or expertise. Position yourself as a subject matter expert and offer tailored solutions and services that address the unique needs and challenges of clients in your niche. By specializing, you can attract higher-value clients, command premium rates, and establish yourself as a leader in your field.

3.2 Geographic Expansion

Expand your reach and grow your client base by exploring opportunities for geographic expansion. Consider expanding your business into new markets or regions where there is demand for bookkeeping services and a lack of competition. Leverage technology and remote work capabilities to serve clients in different locations without the need for physical presence or office space. Invest in marketing and business development initiatives to raise awareness of your services and attract clients in new geographic markets.

3.3 Strategic Partnerships and Alliances

Forge strategic partnerships and alliances with other professionals and service providers in related industries to expand your service offerings and reach new clients. Collaborate with accountants, lawyers, financial advisors, and business consultants to offer integrated solutions and comprehensive services to mutual clients. Build a network of trusted partners and referral sources who can refer clients to you and vice versa, and leverage these relationships to generate leads, expand your client base, and grow your business.

3.4 Innovation and Technology Adoption

Stay ahead of the curve and embrace innovation and technology to drive growth and innovation in your bookkeeping business. Invest in cutting-edge technologies such as cloud accounting software, artificial intelligence, and automation tools to streamline processes, improve efficiency, and deliver value-added services to your clients. Stay updated on emerging trends and technologies in the accounting and finance industry and leverage them to innovate and differentiate your business in the marketplace.

Congratulations! You've explored the exciting possibilities of diversifying your revenue streams beyond traditional bookkeeping services, creating passive income opportunities, and expanding your business horizons to unlock new sources of revenue and growth.

By offering additional services to your clients, creating passive income streams, and exploring new avenues for growth and innovation, you can position yourself for long-term success and sustainability in the dynamic and evolving world of bookkeeping.

So embrace the challenge of diversification, innovation, and expansion, and let your creativity, ambition, and entrepreneurial spirit guide you as you explore new opportunities and chart your course to success. With the right strategies, mindset, and determination, the possibilities are endless for your success and prosperity in the world of bookkeeping and beyond.

Chapter 9: Thriving in Turbulent Times: Adapting to Economic Shifts

Welcome to Chapter 9 of your book, where we delve into the strategies and techniques for thriving in turbulent economic times. In this chapter, we'll explore how to build resilience during economic downturns, pivot your business model to meet changing needs and thrive in an ever-evolving financial landscape. Economic shifts are inevitable, but with the right approach and mindset, you can navigate uncertainty and emerge stronger and more resilient than ever before. So let's dive in and discover how to thrive in turbulent times.

Section 1: Strategies for Resilience During Economic Downturns

Economic downturns are a natural part of the business cycle, but they can pose significant challenges for small businesses, including bookkeeping practices. In this section, we'll explore strategies for building resilience and weathering the storm during economic downturns.

1.1 Build a Financial Buffer

One of the most effective ways to prepare for economic downturns is to build a financial buffer to cushion the impact of reduced revenue and increased expenses. Maintain a healthy cash reserve to cover operating expenses, debt obligations, and emergencies during lean times. Set aside a portion of your revenue each month and prioritize saving and budgeting to build a financial safety net that can sustain your business through economic downturns.

1.2 Diversify Your Client Base

Relying too heavily on a small number of clients can leave your business vulnerable to economic shocks if one or more clients reduce spending or go out of business during a downturn. Diversify your client base by serving clients across different industries, geographic regions, and revenue sizes. Cultivate relationships with a diverse range of clients and industries to spread risk and minimize the impact of economic downturns on your business.

1.3 Focus on Value-Added Services

During economic downturns, clients may become more selective about where they spend their money and may prioritize services that offer tangible value and ROI. Position your bookkeeping practice as a trusted advisor and strategic partner by offering value-added services that help clients save money, increase efficiency, and navigate financial challenges. Focus on services such as financial consulting, tax planning, and strategic planning that provide measurable benefits and address clients' most pressing needs during turbulent times.

1.4 Reduce Overhead and Expenses

When faced with economic uncertainty, it's essential to tighten your belt and reduce overhead and expenses to preserve cash flow and profitability. Review your expenses carefully and identify opportunities to cut costs, streamline operations, and eliminate unnecessary spending. Negotiate with vendors and suppliers for discounts or payment terms, renegotiate leases or contracts to reduce fixed costs, and explore alternative solutions or providers to reduce expenses without sacrificing quality or service.

Section 2: Pivoting Your Business Model for Changing Needs

In times of economic uncertainty, businesses must be agile and adaptable to meet changing needs and market conditions. In this section, we'll explore strategies for pivoting your business model to stay relevant and resilient in turbulent times.

2.1 Identify Emerging Trends and Opportunities

Stay ahead of the curve by identifying emerging trends and opportunities in the market and positioning your business to capitalize on them. Monitor industry trends, consumer preferences, and market dynamics to identify areas of growth and demand. Anticipate changes in client needs and preferences and adapt your service offerings accordingly to meet evolving demands and stay competitive in the marketplace.

2.2 Leverage Technology and Innovation

Technology and innovation can be powerful catalysts for business transformation and growth, especially during times of economic uncertainty. Embrace technology and leverage innovative solutions to streamline processes, improve efficiency, and enhance the customer experience. Invest in cloud accounting software, automation tools, and digital platforms to digitize your operations, reduce manual work, and deliver value-added services to clients in new and innovative ways.

2.3 Expand into Adjacent Markets

Explore opportunities to expand into adjacent markets or diversify your service offerings to capitalize on new revenue streams and growth opportunities. Identify complementary services or industries that align with your core competencies and expertise and leverage your existing client base and relationships to penetrate new markets. Offer bundled services or package deals that provide added value and meet the diverse needs of clients across different industries and sectors.

2.4 Innovate Your Service Delivery Model

Innovate your service delivery model to adapt to changing client preferences and market dynamics. Offer flexible service options, such as virtual consultations, remote support, and on-demand services, to accommodate clients' busy schedules and preferences. Embrace new delivery channels, such as online platforms, mobile apps, and digital marketplaces, to reach clients where they are and deliver services in a convenient and accessible manner.

Section 3: Thriving in an Ever-Evolving Financial Landscape

The financial landscape is constantly evolving, driven by changes in technology, regulation, and consumer behavior. In this section, we'll explore strategies for thriving in an ever-evolving financial landscape and positioning your business for long-term success and sustainability.

3.1 Stay Agile and Adaptive

In a modern moving and dynamic enterprise environment, agility and adaptability are important traits for success. Stay nimble and responsive to changing market conditions, customer preferences, and industry trends. Embrace a culture of innovation and experimentation, and be willing to pivot and iterate your strategies and tactics to stay ahead of the curve and remain competitive in the marketplace.

3.2 Invest in Continuous Learning and Development

Invest in continuous learning and development to stay informed about emerging trends, technologies, and best practices in the accounting and finance industry. Stay updated on changes to tax laws and regulations, accounting standards, and industry developments that may impact your business and clients. Pursue professional development opportunities, such as certifications, training programs, and industry conferences, to enhance your skills and knowledge and position yourself as a trusted advisor and expert in your field.

3.3 Foster Collaboration and Partnerships

Collaboration and partnerships can be powerful drivers of growth and innovation in the financial services industry. Foster strategic alliances with other professionals, service providers, and industry stakeholders to expand your network, access new resources and expertise, and leverage synergies and opportunities for mutual benefit. Collaborate on joint ventures, co-marketing initiatives, and referral programs to expand your reach and attract new clients and opportunities.

3.4 Focus on Client Relationships and Value Creation

In an ever-evolving financial landscape, building strong client relationships and delivering value-added services are key to retaining clients and sustaining long-term success. Focus on understanding your client's needs, preferences, and pain points, and tailor your services and solutions to address their unique challenges and objectives. Provide proactive guidance and advice, communicate openly and transparently, and demonstrate your commitment to delivering exceptional value and service at every touchpoint.

Congratulations! You've explored the strategies and techniques for thriving in turbulent economic times, from building resilience during economic downturns to pivoting your business model for changing needs and thriving in an ever-evolving financial landscape. Economic shifts are inevitable, but with the right approach and mindset, you can navigate uncertainty and emerge stronger and more resilient than ever before.

So embrace the challenge of thriving in turbulent times, and let your creativity, adaptability, and determination guide you as you navigate economic shifts and position your business for long-term success and sustainability. With the right strategies, mindset, and resilience, the possibilities are endless for your success and prosperity in the dynamic and ever-evolving world of bookkeeping and finance.

Chapter 10: The Future of Bookkeeping: Trends and Innovations

Welcome to Chapter 10 of your book, where we delve into the exciting realm of the future of bookkeeping. In this chapter, we'll explore how technological advancements are reshaping the bookkeeping industry, predict future trends that will shape the profession, and discuss strategies for positioning yourself as a leader in the industry. The future of bookkeeping is bright, and by embracing innovation and staying ahead of the curve, you can thrive in the dynamic and evolving landscape of the profession. So let's dive in and explore the future of bookkeeping together.

Section 1: Embracing Technological Advancements in Bookkeeping

Technology is revolutionizing the bookkeeping industry, enabling bookkeepers to streamline processes, improve efficiency, and deliver value-added services to clients. In this section, we'll explore the technological advancements that are reshaping the bookkeeping profession and discuss how you can embrace innovation to stay competitive in the digital age.

1.1 Cloud Accounting Software

Cloud accounting software has transformed the way bookkeepers manage financial data and collaborate with clients. Cloud-based platforms such as QuickBooks Online, Xero, and FreshBooks offer real-time access to financial information, automated data synchronization, and collaborative features that allow bookkeepers and clients to work together seamlessly from anywhere, at any time. Embrace cloud accounting software to streamline workflows, reduce manual work, and deliver timely and accurate financial reporting and insights to clients.

1.2 Artificial Intelligence and Machine Learning

Artificial intelligence (AI) and machine learning are revolutionizing the bookkeeping industry by automating repetitive tasks, analyzing large volumes of data, and uncovering insights and patterns that can inform decision-making. AI-powered tools and algorithms can automate data entry, categorization, and reconciliation, identify anomalies and errors, and provide predictive analytics and forecasting to help clients make informed decisions and optimize performance. Embrace AI and machine learning to enhance productivity, accuracy, and efficiency in your bookkeeping practice and deliver greater value to clients.

1.3 Robotic Process Automation

Robotic process automation (RPA) is transforming the bookkeeping industry by automating routine and rule-based tasks, such as invoice processing, expense management, and payroll processing. RPA software robots can mimic human actions and interact with applications, systems, and data to execute tasks with speed, accuracy, and consistency, freeing up bookkeepers to focus on higher-value activities that require human judgment and expertise. Embrace RPA to automate manual tasks, improve process efficiency, and reduce errors in your bookkeeping practice.

1.4 Blockchain Technology

Blockchain technology is revolutionizing the way financial transactions are recorded, verified, and secured, offering unprecedented transparency, security, and efficiency in bookkeeping and accounting processes. Blockchain-based platforms and distributed ledger technology (DLT) enable secure and immutable recording of transactions, eliminating the need for intermediaries and reducing the risk of fraud and tampering. Embrace blockchain technology to enhance data integrity, transparency, and trust in financial reporting and transactions, and explore opportunities for leveraging blockchain-based solutions in your bookkeeping practice.

Section 2: Predicting Future Trends and Staying Ahead of the Curve

The bookkeeping industry is constantly evolving, driven by technological advancements, regulatory changes, and shifting client needs. In this section, we'll predict future trends that will shape the future of bookkeeping and discuss strategies for staying ahead of the curve and positioning yourself for success in the industry.

2.1 Continued Shift to Cloud-Based Solutions

The adoption of cloud-based solutions will continue to accelerate as bookkeepers and clients embrace the benefits of real-time access, scalability, and collaboration offered by cloud accounting software. In the future, we can expect to see a greater emphasis on cloud-based solutions that integrate seamlessly with other business applications and provide advanced features such as artificial intelligence, machine learning, and predictive analytics to enhance productivity and decision-making.

2.2 Rise of Data Analytics and Business Intelligence

Data analytics and business intelligence will play an increasingly important role in the bookkeeping profession, enabling bookkeepers to analyze large volumes of financial data, uncover insights and trends, and provide valuable strategic guidance and advice to clients. In the future, we can expect to see a greater emphasis on data-driven decision-making, with bookkeepers leveraging advanced analytics tools and techniques to deliver actionable insights and recommendations that drive business growth and performance.

2.3 Focus on Cybersecurity and Data Privacy

With the proliferation of digital technologies and the increasing volume of financial data stored and transmitted online, cybersecurity and data privacy will become paramount concerns for bookkeepers and their clients. In the future, we can expect to see a greater emphasis on cybersecurity measures and data protection strategies to safeguard sensitive financial information from cyber threats, breaches, and attacks. Bookkeepers will need to invest in robust cybersecurity solutions, implement best practices for data security and privacy, and stay informed about emerging threats and vulnerabilities to mitigate risks and protect client data.

2.4 Shift Towards Advisory and Consultative Services

As technology automates routine tasks and processes, bookkeepers will increasingly pivot towards providing advisory and consultative services that deliver strategic value and insights to clients. In the future, we can expect to see a greater emphasis on value-added services such as financial consulting, tax planning, and business advisory, as bookkeepers leverage their expertise and insights to help clients navigate complex financial challenges and achieve their business goals. By focusing on high-value advisory services, bookkeepers can differentiate themselves from automated solutions and position themselves as trusted advisors and strategic partners to their clients.

Section 3: Positioning Yourself as a Leader in the Industry

In a rapidly evolving industry landscape, it's essential to position yourself as a leader and innovator in the bookkeeping profession. In this section, we'll discuss strategies for building your reputation, establishing thought leadership, and staying ahead of the competition in the industry.

3.1 Invest in Continuous Learning and Development

To stay ahead of the curve and maintain a competitive edge in the industry, it's essential to invest in continuous learning and development. Stay updated on the latest trends, technologies, and best practices in the bookkeeping profession by pursuing professional development opportunities, attending industry conferences and events, and engaging in ongoing education and training. By staying informed and up-to-date, you can position yourself as a knowledgeable and authoritative voice in the industry and build credibility and trust with clients and peers.

3.2 Demonstrate Thought Leadership and Expertise

Establish yourself as a thought leader and subject matter expert in the bookkeeping profession by sharing your insights, expertise, and experiences with others. Write articles, blogs, or whitepapers on topics of interest to the industry, participate in webinars or podcasts as a guest speaker or panelist, and contribute to industry publications or forums to showcase your expertise and thought leadership. By sharing valuable content and insights with the community, you can build your reputation, expand your network, and attract new clients and opportunities to your bookkeeping practice.

3.3 Foster Innovation and Collaboration

Embrace innovation and collaboration as key drivers of success in the bookkeeping profession. Foster a culture of innovation within your bookkeeping practice by encouraging creativity, experimentation, and continuous improvement. Collaborate with other professionals, service providers, and industry stakeholders to exchange ideas, share best practices, and explore opportunities for innovation and partnership. By embracing a collaborative and innovative mindset, you can stay ahead of the competition, drive growth and innovation in your practice, and position yourself as a leader in the industry.

3.4 Provide Exceptional Service and Value

Above all, the consciousness of supplying first-rate providers and value
 to your clients to differentiate yourself from competitors and build long-term relationships and loyalty. Listen to your clients' needs, communicate openly and transparently, and deliver high-quality, personalized services that meet and exceed their expectations. By consistently delivering exceptional service and value, you can earn the trust and confidence of your clients, generate positive word-of-mouth referrals, and position yourself as a trusted advisor and partner in their success.

Congratulations! You've explored the future of bookkeeping, from embracing technological advancements to predicting future trends and positioning yourself as a leader in the industry. The future of bookkeeping is bright, and by embracing innovation, staying ahead of the curve, and providing exceptional service and value to clients, you can thrive in the dynamic and evolving landscape of the profession.

So embrace the opportunities and challenges that lie ahead, and let your creativity, innovation, and expertise guide you as you navigate the future of bookkeeping. With the right strategies, mindset, and determination, the possibilities are endless for your success and prosperity in the exciting and ever-evolving world of bookkeeping and accounting.

Conclusion:

Congratulations! You've reached the end of your journey through the world of bookkeeping, where we've explored how anyone can earn six figures from home with a simple bookkeeping business. Throughout this book, we've covered a wide range of topics, from the fundamentals of bookkeeping to the future of the profession, providing you with the knowledge, skills, and strategies You want to achieve this dyn
amic and worthwhile field.

As you reflect on your journey, it's important to celebrate how far you've come and the progress you've made toward achieving your goals. Whether you're just starting on your bookkeeping journey or you're already running a successful practice, remember that success is not just about reaching a destination but about the journey itself – the challenges you've overcome, the lessons you've learned, and the growth you've experienced along the way.

Throughout this book, we've emphasized the importance of mindset, determination, and continuous learning in achieving success in the bookkeeping profession. Success is not guaranteed, and it requires hard work, dedication, and perseverance to overcome obstacles and achieve your goals. But with the right mindset and attitude, combined with the knowledge and skills you've acquired, you have the power to create the life and career you desire.

As you embark on your journey to six figures and beyond, here are some key takeaways to keep in mind:

1. Believe in Yourself
Believe in yourself and your ability to succeed. Confidence is key in entrepreneurship, and having faith in your skills, knowledge, and abilities will empower you to overcome challenges and achieve your goals.

2. Embrace Continuous Learning
Never stop learning and growing. The world of bookkeeping is constantly evolving, and staying updated on the latest trends, technologies, and best practices is essential for staying competitive and positioning yourself for success.

3. Focus on Value Creation
Focus on providing exceptional value to your clients. By delivering high-quality, personalized services that meet and exceed their expectations, you can earn their trust and loyalty and build long-term relationships that drive your success.

4. Adapt to Change

Be adaptable and bendy inside the face of change. The bookkeeping profession is constantly evolving, and embracing change and innovation is essential for staying relevant and thriving in the ever-changing landscape of the industry.

5. Build a Strong Support Network
Surround yourself with a strong support network of mentors, peers, and allies who can provide guidance, advice, and encouragement along your journey. Building relationships and networking with others in the industry can open doors to new opportunities and help you overcome challenges more effectively.

6. Stay Focused on Your Goals
Stay focused on your goals and keep your vision front and center. Set clear, actionable goals for your bookkeeping business and develop a plan to achieve them. Stay disciplined and committed to your goals, and take consistent action towards realizing your dreams.

7. Celebrate Your Successes
Celebrate your successes, no matter how small. Acknowledge and celebrate your achievements and milestones along the way, and use them as motivation to keep pushing forward and striving for even greater success.

As you continue on your journey to six figures and beyond, remember that success is not measured solely by financial wealth, but by the impact you make, the lives you touch, and the legacy you leave behind. Take pride in the work you do, the value you create, and the difference you make in the lives of your clients and community.

So maintain pushing forward, maintain learning, and maintain growing. The journey to six figures and beyond may not always be easy, but with passion, perseverance, and a commitment to excellence, you have the power to achieve your dreams And create the lifestyles and profession you desire.

Thank you for embarking on this journey with me, and I wish you all the success and fulfillment in the world as you continue on your path to success in the exciting and rewarding world of bookkeeping. Here's to your journey to six figures and beyond!

Acknowledgments

The author would like to express gratitude to all those who contributed to the creation and publication of this book, including editors, designers, typesetters, and supporters. Special thanks to Alex A. Aycock for his invaluable guidance and support throughout the writing process.

About the Author

Robert J. White is a seasoned professional with over 5 years of experience in the field of accounting and bookkeeping. With a passion for helping others achieve financial success, Robert J. White has dedicated his career to demystifying complex financial concepts and empowering individuals to take control of their finances.

Robert J. White is a Ph.D. holder and is a certified Accountant with extensive expertise in financial management, analysis, bookkeeping, and reporting. Throughout his career, Robert J. White has worked with businesses of all sizes, from startups to multinational corporations, providing comprehensive accounting and bookkeeping services to help clients achieve their financial goals.

With his book, "Keystrokes to Cash": How Anyone Can Earn Six Figures from Home with a Simple Bookkeeping Business, Robert J. White aims to empower readers to achieve financial fluency and build successful bookkeeping businesses from the comfort of their own homes. Through practical advice, real-world examples, and actionable strategies, he guides readers on a journey toward financial independence and entrepreneurial success.

Robert J. White is excited to share his knowledge and insights with readers and hopes that this book will inspire and empower individuals to unlock their full potential and create the life and career they desire. Whether you're just starting on your bookkeeping journey or looking to take your business to the next level, his book provides the guidance and inspiration you need to achieve your goals and thrive in the world of bookkeeping.

www.ingramcontent.com/pod-product-compliance
Lightning Source LLC
Chambersburg PA
CBHW050319230526
45471CB00005B/2264